**For Beatrix, Harrison, Akiva,
and seeds sown –R.P.**

For Tien and Reid –M.A.

Text copyright © 2018 by Rubin Pfeffer
Jacket art and interior illustrations copyright © 2018 by Mike Austin

All rights reserved. Published in the United States by Random House Children's Books,
a division of Penguin Random House LLC, New York.

Random House and the colophon are registered trademarks of Penguin Random House LLC.

Visit us on the Web! rhcbooks.com

Educators and librarians, for a variety of teaching tools, visit us at RHTeachersLibrarians.com

Library of Congress Cataloging-in-Publication Data is available upon request.
ISBN 978-1-5247-1464-2 (trade) — ISBN 978-1-5247-1465-9 (lib. bdg.) — ISBN 978-1-5247-1466-6 (ebook)

MANUFACTURED IN CHINA
10 9 8 7 6 5 4 3 2 1
First Edition

SUMMER SUPPER

by Rubin Pfeffer

pictures by Mike Austin

Random House 🏠 New York

Sticks

String

Shovel soil.

Sun

Sow seeds.

Snail

Sprinkle,

sprinkle.

Stem

SQUIRM, SQUIRM

stalk.

Sunflower

Scarecrow

Snip,

snip, snip.

Sweet

STRAWBERRIES

SPUDS

Sample.

SPINACH

SALE!

SCALE

Sell.

Slice. Soak.

Shuck.

Steam

Skillet

Stove

Sizzle, swirl,

SECRET SAUCE

Salt shaker

swish, SAUTÉ!

Shake
Shake

Sprinkle spice.

Stir salad.

Sniff, sniff . . .

SUCCOTASH!

smell.

Derry Public Library

Sippy
Straw
Slurp!

SUPPER!

Shimmy,

Sponge

Suds

Scrub.

Soap

Stack

Save. Store.

Snooze.

Shhh . . .

Slice

SNACK!